Inspirational Poems with Power

by Debbie Baker

Copyright 2017

ALL RIGHTS RESERVED

No part of this work may be reproduced or transmitted in any form or by any means, whether electronic or mechanical, including photocopying and recording, or by any information storage or retrieval system without the proper written permission of the copyright owner.

ISBN: 978-0-692-04498-8

Front cover image, *Sunday*, used by permission of Lane Gower.

Table of Contents

Heaven or Hell	2
Power Upon the Cross	4
In the Army of the Lord	6
Parable	8
His Command	10
I Am	12
The Cross	14
A Man Called Jesus	16
Eternal Life	18
Righteouness	20
My Creed to Salvation	22
Jesus Knows	24
About the Poet	26

Heaven or Hell

Torn apart the skies heaven or hell
But down below the devil dwells
All good things are from a heavenly host
And of all things God wants us to love Him the most
We all pray for everlasting life, in the light
To never again be in the darkness of night
Doubt, confusion, hatred and fear
Are all things the devil holds dear
Now on this path we have choices to make
And it's up to you which path to take.

Power Upon the Cross

The symbol of the power on the cross through the Bible has been seen
Here are three stories to tell you what I mean
First, there on the shore stands Moses at the Red Sea
With rod in one hand stretched his arms to Thee
As he cried out, God placed power in his hand
To save the Israelites, to lead them to the promised land
Second, through locks of his hair, divine strength Samson was given
He overcame his enemies, with power he was driven
Samson prayed to God, "Remember me, strengthen me once more."
As he pulled two pillars together crashing the temple to the floor
And third, made powerful upon the cross, with power that only God can give
With arms open wide Jesus's life was sacrificed so that we all may live

And God said, "It is finished"
John 19:30

In the Army of the Lord

Strapped for battle onward we fight
On the battle field with the enemy in sight
Preparing yourselves in the Word, which is your sword
As you look to the hills which comes your help from
    the Lord
Extinguish arrows of evil with all your will
By trusting in God, your faith and your shield
Fasten the truth around your waist like a belt
While standing victoriously on God's grace it can be felt
Jesus is your helmet of Salvation, protector from the
    deeds of darkness
As you battle things inhuman, evil and heartless
Upon this breastplate the enemy will know
Therein, filled with righteousness, is a Godly flow
So with each piece of armor, for God we stand
With feet fitted for the gospel of peace, all across
    this land.

Parable

By what they see is blind
Eyes closed to the Divine
To live is all in me
My soul, content and free
Christ my shepherd, me in the flock
Strong in the spirit, evil can't block
Jesus said, "To look upon me is to look upon the Father"
Me a child of God, I am his daughter
For what is it, the faith of a mustard seed?
To live for God, that's all you need.

His Command

In the mist of the calmness, your voice I seek
With the wind through the trees you do speak
No worries or problems are at hand
Steadfast to My word on this He commands
For all that you need is in Me
Have patience and you will see
Remember whom you love the most
God! Father! Son! and The Holy Ghost!

I Am

I Am is whom the Bible speaks of
Lacking understanding of my Father above
Moses asks, "For whom do I speak?"
I Am, I Am the God you seek.
Adulteress Samaritan, exposed in her sin
I Am condemns not, go and sin not again
The Covenant Keeper to Isaac, Jacob, and Abraham
Living Water, Light of the World, I Am
Living God, I Am, tempted by the devil himself
With promises of worldly things and wealth
So as of now there is no doubt who I must be
I Am, I Am Savior of Souls who can set you free.

The Cross

On the cross was our King
People stood around not doing a thing
In the middle hung Jesus between a liar and a thief
On one side a nonbeliever and on the other—one who
 believes
With a crown of thorns they placed on His head
Around about His face He bled
Mockery they made of His name
I am the "Son of God" He proclaimed
Blasphemy, blasphemy it's lies that you say
Crowned with thorns they nailed him to the cross
 that day
As they pierced Him in His side they stood in a daze
By what they saw they all were amazed
Weeping and mourning at the foot of the cross
The Lord our Savior paid the cost
King of the Jews the one they hold dear
Crucified the wrong man now they have fear
For your sins and mine he bare
Our souls Jesus asks God to spare
Remember, on the cross was our Lord, for all to see
Just how our Savior died to set us all free.

A Man Called Jesus

He healed the sick made the blind to see
Touched the hearts and minds of many, put them at
    peace and set them free
With love unconditional and never an evil thought in
    his head
He fed five thousand men, women, and children with two
    fish and five loaves of bread
He gave his life; He bore the sins for us
There on the cross the Messiah, a man called Jesus.

Eternal Life

He asks no questions and gives no reason
There is a time and everything has its season
With understanding, death is nothing to fear
But a celebration of life, knowing God is near.
True rest comes only to those who believe
Today, hear His voice and never again be deceived
So unsure is this doubting Thomas!
But with faith and patience, we'll inherit the promise

Righteousness

Entering the gates of heaven, there are somethings you
    will need
A state of moral perfection, righteousness indeed
Through efforts of our own, righteousness we cannot
    achieve
You must have faith in our Lord Jesus Christ and believe
He took it upon himself, punishment for all mankind
For that reason we should seek God's righteousness,
    make it our priority in life to find
That righteousness through Jesus Christ is given free
And it establishes our relationship with God you see
Remember, having faith for what Christ has done for us
We obtain the gift of righteousness from God, in whom
    we trust